CURSIVE WRITING
Joining Letters

Ages: 4-6 years

This book belongs to

MOONSTONE

Joining Letters

Trace the letters with a pencil. Then practice writing the letters on the lines.

aa   bb   cc   dd

aa   bb   cc   dd

aa   bb   cc   dd

aa   bb   cc   dd

Joining Letters

Trace the letters with a pencil. Then practice writing the letters on the lines.

ee   ff   gg   hh

ee   ff   gg   hh

ee   ff   gg   hh

ee   ff   gg   hh

Joining Letters

Trace the letters with a pencil. Then practice writing the letters on the lines.

ii	jj	kk	ll

ii jj kk ll

ii jj kk ll

ii jj kk ll

Joining Letters

Trace the letters with a pencil. Then practice writing the letters on the lines.

mm	nn	oo	pp
mm	nn	oo	pp
mm	nn	oo	pp
mm	nn	oo	pp

Joining Letters

Trace the letters with a pencil. Then practice writing the letters on the lines.

| qq | rr | ss | tt |

qq   rr   ss   tt

qq   rr   ss   tt

qq   rr   ss   tt

Joining Letters

u – x

Trace the letters with a pencil. Then practice writing the letters on the lines.

uu   uv   uuu   xx

Joining Letters

Trace the letters with a pencil. Then practice writing the letters on the lines.

yy   zz

yy   zz

yy   zz

yy   zz

Trace the letters with a pencil. Then practice writing the letters on the lines.

| an | at | ab | ac |

an   *at*   *ab*   *ac*

an   *at*   *ab*   *ac*

an   *at*   *ab*   *ac*

Joining Letters

Trace the letters with a pencil. Then practice writing the letters on the lines.

| ba | bb | bc | bd |

| ba | bb | bc | bd |

| ba | bb | bc | bd |

| ba | bb | bc | bd |

Joining Letters

Trace the letters with a pencil. Then practice writing the letters on the lines.

ca   cm   cg   ch

ca   cm   cg   ch

ca   cm   cg   ch

ca   cm   cg   ch

Joining Letters

Trace the letters with a pencil. Then practice writing the letters on the lines.

| df | dv | dk | dt |

| df | dv | dk | dt |

| df | dv | dk | dt |

| df | dv | dk | dt |

Joining Letters

Trace the letters with a pencil. Then practice writing the letters on the lines.

ea   ec   em   ez

ea   ec   em   ez

ea   ec   em   ez

ea   ec   em   ez

Joining Letters

Trace the letters with a pencil. Then practice writing the letters on the lines.

fc   fa   fk   fp

fc   fa   fk   fp

fc   fa   fk   fp

fc   fa   fk   fp

Joining Letters

Trace the letters with a pencil. Then practice writing the letters on the lines.

ge	go	gu	gh

ge   go   gu   gh

ge   go   gu   gh

ge   go   gu   gh

15

Joining Letters

Trace the letters with a pencil. Then practice writing the letters on the lines.

| ha | hb | hc | hd |

ha   hb   hc   hd

ha   hb   hc   hd

ha   hb   hc   hd

Joining Letters

Trace the letters with a pencil. Then practice writing the letters on the lines.

it	in	ig	ip
it	in	ig	ip
it	in	ig	ip
it	in	ig	ip

Joining Letters

Trace the letters with a pencil. Then practice writing the letters on the lines.

jc   jn   jo   jt

jc   jn   jo   jt

jc   jn   jo   jt

jc   jn   jo   jt

Joining Letters

Trace the letters with a pencil. Then practice writing the letters on the lines.

kc	km	kg	kr

kc   km   kg   kr

kc   km   kg   kr

kc   km   kg   kr

Joining Letters

Trace the letters with a pencil. Then practice writing the letters on the lines.

lm	lg	lz	lc
lm	lg	lz	lc
lm	lg	lz	lc
lm	lg	lz	lc

Joining Letters

Trace the letters with a pencil. Then practice writing the letters on the lines.

| ma | mc | mp | mn |

ma   mc   mp   mn

ma   mc   mp   mn

ma   mc   mp   mn

Joining Letters

Trace the letters with a pencil. Then practice writing the letters on the lines.

| na | ng | ng | nd |

na ng ng nd

na ng ng nd

na ng ng nd

Joining Letters

Trace the letters with a pencil. Then practice writing the letters on the lines.

| or | oi | oa | ob |

or   oi   oa   ob

or   oi   oa   ob

or   oi   oa   ob

Joining Letters

Trace the letters with a pencil. Then practice writing the letters on the lines.

| pa | pr | pc | pg |

pa   pr   pc   pg

pa   pr   pc   pg

pa   pr   pc   pg

Trace the letters with a pencil. Then practice writing the letters on the lines.

qa	qr	qc	qg

qa   qr   qc   qg

qa   qr   qc   qg

qa   qr   qc   qg

Joining Letters

Trace the letters with a pencil. Then practice writing the letters on the lines.

| rd | rc | rn | rg |

rd   rc   rn   rg

rd   rc   rn   rg

rd   rc   rn   rg

Joining Letters

Trace the letters with a pencil. Then practice writing the letters on the lines.

sg	sn	so	sf

sg   sn   so   sf

sg   sn   so   sf

sg   sn   so   sf

Joining Letters

Trace the letters with a pencil. Then practice writing the letters on the lines.

to	tn	td	tf
to	tn	td	tf
to	tn	td	tf
to	tn	td	tf

Joining Letters

Trace the letters with a pencil. Then practice writing the letters on the lines.

up   ur   un   us

up   ur   un   us

up   ur   un   us

up   ur   un   us

Joining Letters

Trace the letters with a pencil. Then practice writing the letters on the lines.

nr   ni   ng   no

nr   ni   ng   no

nr   ni   ng   no

nr   ni   ng   no

Joining Letters

Trace the letters with a pencil. Then practice writing the letters on the lines.

wc   we   wi   wr

wc   we   wi   wr

Joining Letters

Trace the letters with a pencil. Then practice writing the letters on the lines.

xa   xb   xc   xd

xa   xb   xc   xd

Joining Letters

Trace the letters with a pencil. Then practice writing the letters on the lines.

yg yc yn yk

yg yc yn yk

Joining Letters

Trace the letters with a pencil. Then practice writing the letters on the lines.

za zk zp zs

za zk zp zs